Withering West

Letter to Idiots Who Shift Blame for Their Decline on Immigrants and Muslims

Muhammad Hanif

Withering West

Letter to Idiots Who Shift Blame for Their Decline on Immigrants and Muslims

First Edition - May 2019

© Copyright 2018 Muhammad Hanif

All Rights Reserved

Disclaimer

This is a work of fiction. The names and characters are either the products of writer's imagination or used in a fictitious way. Any resemblance to actual persons, living or dead is purely coincidental. Any real names of objects or places that may be found have been used in a fictitious way to write the stories or poems and the author is not responsible for any use of that information, or any other information in this book by the readers and its consequences thereof, if any.

Dedication

This is dedicated to the wise people in the West who may still have the ability to think and take positive actions to help sustain life for all those who love life, regardless of colour, race, religion, and any and every other kind of prejudice.

Books by this Author

1. **Advice for Life**
2. **Clown and Frown**
3. **East and West – Home is the Best, An Immigrant's Feelings and Views, A Poem**
4. **Everyday Poems**
5. **Little Donkey**
6. **Living With a Stiff spine**
7. **Naughty Lioness (A Novel)**
8. **Our World - Observations**
9. **Short Stories Acrostic Way**
10. **Withering West - Letter to Idiots Who Shift Blame for Their Decline on Immigrants and Muslims**
11. **Acrostic Stories Work Book - Companion to Short Stories Acrostic Way**

Table of Contents

Introduction 7

Withering West.................................13

Notes: 23

Introduction

Here is what people in the West need to ask themselves and to think, if they can, which I believe that they can, before they blame the reasons for their systematic decline on everybody else other than themselves. It has become a fashion to blame the causes of the decline of the West on the religion of Islam and Muslim immigrants, and people who are not White.

These are the escape goats in general and a significant indication of the mental decline of the West, which is responsible for the decline of the West in general and decline and deterioration of the countries and societies elsewhere in the Eastern World, in particular.

It is also true that these people from other lands may be contributing to this decline in a small way but the responsibility and the fundamental reasons for decline of the West are deeply rooted in the West itself, and those blaming the others for this phenomenon.

The West is abdicating its responsibility by blaming others for faults of their own.

The West did not achieve anything without having terrorised the world for centuries and robbing and raping other Nations.

And because now that possibility has declined and has almost vanished, the West finds itself run out of ideas to maintain and sustain, whatever progress, they had made and values they adored, which were at the cost of lives of Billions of other people.

The West in fact never had any constructive and sustainable ideas, except the one of using brute force, which they used and exercised mercilessly.

Now, the West pretends to be the most Civilized People, and portray the Nations that they destroyed and robbed, as beasts.

The West needs to look in the mirror and ask itself, if it is indeed capable of doing anything constructive, other than having been a beast for centuries, and still continuing to be so in a diplomatic way.

Their WEST Credit Card for enjoying unlimited freedom to

destroy other countries and live off their wealth has long expired.

They have to either do something constructive to renew it or just declare moral, mental and physical bankruptcy and cease to exist as an entity they have known for the past several centuries, and go back to the dark ages before disappearing permanently, as the possibility of that exists because of the West's own doing, its bad behaviour, and digging its own grave, while having done that for other societies, cultures and Nations.

May be, the WEST should punish all the other Nations and their people whom they blame for the West's downfall with Nuclear Weapons and make sure that all countries are destroyed completely, that are NON WHITE, and as well as the MUSLIM countries and then the WEST CAN LIVE HAPPILY for the rest of their lives.

I hope that things will improve as I believe that there are always people who can, and who are capable of doing better things, if they want.

Author

May 13, 2019

Withering West

Letter to Idiots on their Decline

Just ask yourself the questions listed here and then write down the answers to them.

1. Why Alexander went to destroy Nations in the Middle East, and the Indian Sub-Continent (South Asia)?

2. Why the Dutch, Portuguese, French, and The English go to India?

3. Why did the French fight in Indo-China (Vietnam)?

4. Why did the USA fight in Indo-China (Vietnam)? What did it achieve?

5. Why did the British stay in India?

6. What are the French proud of? They were beaten in Europe, India, Indo-China and you should know what happened to them in North America?

7. Why the USA did not throw an Atom Bomb on Germany but had no hesitation in throwing it on Japan?

8. Why did USA go to war with Iraq twice and that too on lies and false pretenses?

9. If USSR was an enemy (Laugh) then why did USA help them in WWII and bullied Iran in the process?

10. Why USA did not throw Atom Bomb on USSR on their adventures in Europe, in other Republics in Central Asia, and in 1979, when USSR invaded Afghanistan?

11. Why a Conservative Prime Minister of Canada could not spare a million dollars for a business exhibit in South Korea, but could spend hundreds of Millions of dollars to bomb Libya and then say, "We won the war?"

12.   Why USA was dying to support the rebels in Libya and it could not even find them?

13.   Why USA bombed Libya?

14.   Do you know that none of the three religions (Judaism, Christianity, and Islam) had anything to do with the West?

15.   Do you know that the Arab can be a Jew, a Christian, A Muslim or an Atheist?

16.   Do you know that whereas you pretend to hate Hitler, most of you like him and would like to follow him?

17. Why KKK is not considered and treated like a terrorist organization?

18. Why it is so that everything WEST does is part of the Freedom of Speech or Expression but when someone else says or does the same thing then you call it a Hate Speech or Hate crime?

19. Why are some drugs like Marijuana being legalized? Will it not impact driving or general social behaviour?

20. Why smoking of tobacco or cigarettes is banned (it should be banned) which are not the cause of an accident after smoking one or

a few but alcohol is not banned which does cause impairment and accidents by those who consume it?

21. Why do you allow people to migrate to your countries in the West if you do not like them?

22. Why do you allow people to migrate to your countries in the West if you do not like their religion?

23. Why do you allow people to migrate to your countries in the West if you do not like their customs?

24. Why do you let refugees come in when you know that they are indeed not refugees?

25.   Why many countries in the WEST allowed people and still allow people to migrate to your countries because you needed people in IT and other technologies?

You pretend to be more advanced than the countries these people were/are coming from, so could it be that you are incompetent, inefficient or just plain stupid, that you could not train and educate your own manpower, and then you make life miserable for those who came?

26.   If you are indeed advanced then why you were not able to produce trained and qualified people in your own homelands?

27.   Why people who were already here were not given the opportunity for those jobs where you imported people from Third World Countries, or other countries, even though many were qualified and experienced right here (in the West)?

28.   Why the WEST is so full of hate that people throw stones and express hate by calling slurs, misbehaving and putting down, once an immigrant of a better colour is here with proper documents etc.?

29.   Do you know that the white man (woman) is well respected in almost all Non White Countries and people go out of the way to help and

accommodate them and the White man (woman) most of the times abuses those hospitalities, but no non-white expects such behaviour from the Whites, but at the same time they do not expect bad behaviour either?

30.   Why did the Romans ruled in the Middle East?

31.   Why did the black slave trade exist in USA?

32.   Why did the Whites go to South Africa and treated the people in the worst possible manner?

33.   Why every single country in Africa was a victim of the Whites?

34.   Why are they (WEST) selling citizenships for large sums of money to people of the countries that they do not like?

35.   Why do the countries in the West lower requirements for citizenship and then increase or change?

36.   Are Whites or the WEST not a terrorist entity – a super terrorist?

37.   Has the White (WEST) ever passed the basic need of survival – the need for food and shelter?

38.   Can you understand that you, the West, are the problem?

Notes:

28

About the Author

Muhammad Hanif has various interests and he is passionate about writing. He also likes to travel. His educational background includes studies in science, psychology, computer science and business. He is working on several book writing projects which includes writing biography, self-help or advice, acrostic stories, some poetry and fiction.

Books by this Author

1. **Advice for Life**
2. **Clown and Frown**
3. **East and West – Home is the Best, An Immigrant's Feelings and Views, A Poem**
4. **Everyday Poems**
5. **Little Donkey**
6. **Living With a Stiff spine**
7. **Naughty Lioness (A Novel)**
8. **Our World - Observations**
9. **Short Stories Acrostic Way**
10. **Withering West - Letter to Idiots Who Shift Blame for Their Decline on Immigrants and Muslims**
11. **Acrostic Stories Work Book - Companion to Short Stories Acrostic Way**